Paula J. Albano

Title:

"MASTERING THE CHESSBOARD: The Strategic Power Of Negotiation

Paula J. Albano

Paula J. Albano

TABLE OF CONTENT

INTRODUCTION

In a realm where words dance with intentions and silence harmonizes with implicit issues, the art of concession emerges as an enigmatic ballet of mortal commerce. Like the gentle eclipse and inflow of the ocean runs, negotiating is neither solely about cession nor domination, but about the intricate choreography of understanding, persuasion, and collective agreement. Shoveling into the strategic power of concession is akin to embarking on a mystical trip where every discussion becomes an implicit oil for painting the masterpiece of concession. With this title, we shall not simply bandy tactics and ways, but wander through the metaphysical tapestries of mortal connections, where the spoken, implied, seen, and unseen meet in the theater of concession.

In a world where the whispers of the wind intertwine with the solicitations of the soul, concession stands as the ethereal ground between the realm of dreams and the sphere of reality.

Paula J. Albano

It's not just an act, but a cosmic cotillion of powers, where words come warbles and pauses echo with the unsaid. The strategic power of concession is not simply a tool in the magazine of the worldly wise, but a sacred ritual where fates are rewritten, not with the muscle of a pen, but with the meter of dialogue. Through this title, we drift beyond the palpable and touch the indefinable, weaving through a maze where reason meets suspicion, and pragmatism waltzes with magic. Prepare to trip beyond the robe of the mundane, into the Jeremiah heart of concession's ethereal substance.

In the Elysian theater where stars discourse in the language of light and worlds trill the ocean, there lies the nebulous realm of concession. It's not just a converse between mortals, but an ancient witchcraft where souls change fractions of cosmic dreams. The strategic power of concession is the esoteric key to unleashing doors, where realities blend and fantasies extend their bodies. Then, sense dissolves into stardust and strategies come moonlit sonatas. With this title, we'll embark on an odyssey, not through the corridors of convention, but soaring on the puffs of imagination. Dive into the opalescent waters of the unknown, and let the symphony of the macrocosm guide our converse beyond the midairs of appreciation.

In the outstanding shade of intellectual hobbies, nestled amidst the vestments of gospel and the tinges of abstract study, lies the enigmatic realm of concession. The strategic power of concession, transcending the rambler boundaries of bare dialogue, emerges as a symphony of cerebral complications. It's neither solely an exchange nor a bare sale, but rather a ballet of abstract dynamics and metaphysical undertones. With this title, we aren't probing into a bare subject, but navigating the complicated corridors of study, where empiricism gracefully curvatures to the nuances of the intangible. We invite compendiums to transcend the concrete, venturing into a disquisition of the sublime confines of concession's more ethereal angles.

Paula J. Albano

CHAPTER ONE

THE ROLE OF NEGOTIATION IN MODERN TIMES

"The Role of Negotiation in Modern Times: A Whimsical Reflection"
In the moment's chromatic period, where digital rainbows meet analog dreams, concession has evolved from bare dialogue into a lyrical ballet danced on the world's stage.

1. ** Starry- eyed Globalization ** In a world where land masses are barely incremental on virtual platforms, concession is our passport to the fantastical land of' GlobalVille'. It's lower about trade agreements and farther about trading tales of wonder.

2. ** Politic conceits ** When political leaders sit across starlit tables, it isn't just about resolving difficulties. They're casting tales for the grand storybook of humanity.

3. **Eco-Ethereal exchanges ** As nature whispers its secrets and woe, nations gather, not just to negotiate but to decipher the songs sung by the winds.

4. ** Technological Tapestries ** In the shimmering realm of bones
and bottoms, lodgment determine which digital unicorns we ride and which cyber- dragons we befriend.

5. ** Cultural Constellations ** concession is the artist oil painting vibrant strokes of understanding across the oil painting of our different world, blending colors of tradition and invention.

6. ** Factory cautions ** Forget boardrooms; the modern concession arena is a magical timber where ideas flutter like luminescent butterflies, seeking the perfect place to land.

7. ** Consumer Chronicles ** moment's paperback doesn't just pick a product; they embark on a grand adventure. Every concession is a chapter in their legend.

In the capricious theater of modern times, concession isn't just strategy; it's fabricator, dream-weaving, and star- shadowing. It's how we script the charming chronicles of our connected creation.

WHY STRATEGY MATTERS IN NEGOTIATION
** Why Strategy Matters in concession A Capricious Dive **

In the mystical realm of concession, where words come magic spells and handshakes seal fates, strategy is the transported map guiding moneybags through treacherous conversational timbers.

1. ** Charting Starry pretensions ** Strategy is the North Star, guiding drifters towards shimmering dreams and moonlit objects, icing they don't wander into conversational snares.

2. ** Weaving Protective Spells ** A keen strategy conjures protective charms, guarding intercessors from the surprise hexes and curses of counterarguments.

3. ** decrypting Enigmatic Opponents ** With strategy's magical lens, one can regard into the other party's heart, unveiling their deepest wishes and subtlest fears, dancing in shadow and light.

4. ** Applying Conversational Wands ** Strategy bestows intercessors with wands that control the cadence of dialogue, icing they lead the ballet of words with grace.

5. ** Guarding Against Dragon risks ** In the changeable land of concession, strategy is the guard against fire- breathing challenges, icing safe passage through coarse difficulties.

6. ** Savoring Time's elixirs ** With strategy's potion, moments come meaningful, icing that every crack of the timer drips with purpose and energy.

7. ** Casting transported Alliances ** further than just deal- making, a strategic alchemist seeks to blend collaborative dreams into a golden potion of cooperation.

8. ** Building islets of shafts ** Beyond the immediate quest, strategy weaves moonlit islets, connecting hearts and icing future magical rendezvous.

9. ** Calming Tempestuous Hearts ** Strategy, like a soothing lullaby, keeps passions from stirring storms, icing the swell of concession and remaining tranquil.

10. ** soliciting comforting issues ** At the trip's end, strategy ensures that both moneybags uncover hidden treasures, feeling like titleholders of their shared tale.

In the capricious theater of concession, strategy isn't just a plan; it's the magic carpet, the compass, and the guiding starlight, weaving tales of success in the grand shade of dialogue.

FOUNDATIONS OF CONCESSION

** Foundations of concession **

1. ** Preparation and Planning ** Before entering a concession, one must be well- prepared. This includes understanding your own position, knowing your objects, and anticipating the conditions and wants of the other party.

2. ** Relationship structure ** Successful lodging constantly depends on the quality of the relationship between the parties. Trust, respect, and collaborative understanding can pave the way for further fruitful exchanges.

3. ** Active listening ** This is further than just hearing words. It's about understanding and interpreting the underpinning passions, enterprises, and provocations of the other party.

4. ** Effective Communication ** fluently conveying your perspective, while being open to feedback, is vital. This avoids misinterpretations and helps in erecting a collaborative terrain.

5. ** Questioning Chops ** Asking the right questions can give precious perceptivity, helping you understand the other party's position and meaning areas of common interest or implicit concession.

6. ** Win- Win intelligence ** Aim for results that benefit all parties involved. rather than viewing concession as a zero- sum game, consider it a collaborative trouble to find collaborative benefits.

7. ** Problem- working Approach ** concentrate on addressing the root causes of dissensions, rather than sticking to rigid positions. This involves brainstorming and creativity.

8. ** strictness ** Being adaptable in your approach allows you to navigate the changeable waters of concession, making it easier to find common ground.

9. ** Understanding Power Dynamics ** recognize the power balance in a concession. Whether it's predicated on information, position, or resources, understanding power dynamics helps in strategizing effectively.

10. ** Ethical morals ** Uphold integrity and honesty. Ethical lodgings make long- term trust and foster sustainable connections.

11. ** Emotional Intelligence ** Being suitable to manage and interpret passions, both yours and the other party's, is vital. This helps in addressing enterprises genuinely and avoiding reactive conduct.

12. ** ending and Commitment ** Once an agreement is reached, ensure both parties understand and commit to the terms. Clear documentation and follow- up are pivotal to successful performance.

At its core, concession is about bridging differences to reach collaborative agreement. These foundations serve as guiding principles, icing that the process is both effective and dutiful.

Paula J. Albano

CHAPTER TWO

BASICS OF EFFECTIVE COMMUNICATION

Then are the basics of effective communication in a terse manner

1. ** Clarity ** Be clear about what you want to convey. Avoid slang unless your followership understands it.
2. ** Active harkening ** hear to understand, not just to respond. This helps in erecting collective respect.
3. ** Empathy ** Put yourself in the other person's shoes to understand their perspective more.
4. ** Open- mindedness ** Be open to feedback and different shoes.
5. ** Body Language ** ensure that your body language aligns with your words. Avoid crossed arms or lack of eye contact.
6. ** Be Present ** concentrate on the current discussion without distractions.
7. ** Feedback ** Regularly seek feedback to ensure the communication is understood.
8. ** Tone of Voice ** Be aware of how you are speaking, not just what you are saying.
9. ** Brevity ** Keep it short and to the point, especially in professional settings.

10. ** Structure ** Organize your studies before you communicate. This can be done by having a clear morning, middle, and end to your communication.

11. ** Avoid hypotheticals ** Do not assume you know what the other person is allowing or feeling.

12. ** Rigidity ** Acclimate your communication style grounded on your followership and situation.

Learning these basics will greatly enhance the effectiveness of your communication in colorful settings.

UNDERSTANDING COLLECTIVE INTERESTS

clearly! Then is a terse explanation of understanding collective interests in accommodations

** Understanding collective Interests in Accommodations **

1. ** description ** collective interests relate to participated benefits or common pretensions between negotiating parties. relating these can produce palm- palm situations.

2. ** significance ** By understanding and fastening on collective interests, accommodations can move from competitive stations(win- lose) to cooperative bones
(palm- palm). This can affect further durable and salutary agreements for both parties.

3. ** Discovery ** To uncover collective interests
- Ask open- concluded questions.
- hear laboriously to the other party's enterprises and requirements.
- Partake your own requirements and objects without revealing your nethermost line precociously.

4. ** Building Trust ** Honest and open dialogue fosters trust, making it easier to identify and prioritize collective interests.

5. ** Expand the Pie ** rather than dividing being coffers, find ways to produce further value for both parties. This can be done by brainstorming and being open to innovative results.

6. ** Avoid hypotheticals ** Do not presume to know the other party's interests. What might feel insignificant to you could be pivotal for them, and vice versa.

7. ** Common Ground ** Establishing collective interests can serve as a foundation or common ground, indeed when there are points of disagreement.

8. ** Long- Term Perspective ** Fasting on collective interests can lead to stronger long- term connections and repeat collaborations, as parties view each other as mates rather than adversaries.

By centering accommodations around collective interests, parties can more effectively navigate dissensions , find innovative results, and make lasting, salutary agreements.

PRINCIPLES OF STRATEGIC NEGOTIATION

clearly! Then are the principles of strategic concession

1. ** Preparation ** Completely probe the other party, their interests, objects, and implicit druthers
before entering into accommodations. This empowers you with precious information to make informed opinions.

2. ** Clear objects ** Define your pretensions and precedences for the concession. Having a clear understanding of what you want to achieve helps guide your strategy.

3. ** Inflexibility ** Be set to acclimatize your approach grounded on new information or changing circumstances during the concession process.

4. ** Active harkening ** Pay close attention to what the other party is saying. hear not only to the words, but also to the underpinning interests and enterprises they express.

5. ** collective Gain ** Strive for palm- palm issues by relating and fastening on common interests that can profit both parties. This promotes collaboration and strengthens connections.

6. ** BATNA ** Know your Stylish Indispensable to a Negotiated Agreement(BATNA). This is your fallback plan if accommodations fail. It provides a standard for assessing the value of the current deal.

7. ** Creating Value ** Seek openings to expand the pie and produce further value for both parties. This can involve innovative results that address both sides' requirements.

8. ** Timing ** Understand when to be patient and when to push for progress. Timing can play a significant part in accommodations.

9. ** Emotional Intelligence ** Manage your feelings and be attuned to the feelings of the other party. Emotional mindfulness can impact the concession atmosphere.

10. ** Building Rapport ** Establishing fellowship and erecting a positive relationship can ameliorate communication, trust, and the overall concession climate.

11. ** Information participating ** Partake applicable information strategically to make trust and demonstrate commitment to changing a mutually salutary agreement.

12. ** Concessions ** Plan your concessions precisely. Each concession should be tied to a gain, and they should be given incrementally.

13. ** Ethics ** Maintain ethical geste
 throughout the concession process. Trust and credibility are critical for successful accommodations.

14. **Post-Negotiation Evaluation ** After the concession, review the process and outgrowth to identify assignments learned and areas for enhancement.

By following these principles, you can approach accommodations strategically, increase the liability of achieving favorable issues, and make stronger connections with your counterparts.

Paula J. Albano

CHAPTER THREE

PRE-NEGOTIATION RESEARCH AND PREPARATION

 Pre-negotiation exploration and medication is the root done before entering any concession, icing you are equipped with vital information and a clear strategy. Then there is a breakdown
1. ** Self- Assessment **
- ** objects ** Define your primary pretensions and secondary objects. Determine what you absolutely need and what you are willing to compromise on.

- ** Limitations ** Identify your walk- away point or the point at which you would choose not to do the deal.

 2. ** Understanding the Other Party **

- ** Background ** exploration the history, character, fiscal health, and once geste of the party you are negotiating with.

 - ** objects and Needs ** Anticipate their primary pretensions and implicit concessions.

 - ** Implicit Pressure Points ** Identify areas where they might be particularly motivated to reach an agreement.

 3. ** Market Research **

- probe the broader request or terrain girding the concession. Understand standard practices, pricing, or any recent changes in the geography.

 4. ** BATNA(Best Alternative to a Negotiated Agreement) **

 - Establish your BATNA. This is your fallback option if the concession does not yield a satisfactory result.

- Consider the other party's BATNA. It'll give perceptivity into their possible conduct and opinions.

 5. ** Plan Concessions **

- Decide in advance what you're willing to give up and prioritize these concessions. - suppose about implicit trade- offs that might profit both parties.

 6. ** Strategic Approach **

- Decide on your concession style cooperative(palm- palm), competitive(win- lose), or nearly in between.

- Develop a general roadmap for how you fantasize the concession proceeding. 7. ** Anticipate expostulations **

- Predict implicit enterprises or expostulations the other party might have and prepare responses.

8. ** Cultural Sensitivity **

- If negotiating with someone from a different artistic background, explore artistic morals and form to avoid misconstructions.

 9. ** Logistical Medications ** - Choose an applicable venue, insure all needed accouterments and attestation are set, and set an docket if applicable.

10. ** Practice **

- If possible, part- play the concession with a coworker or trainer. This can punctuate unlooked-for challenges and give you a chance to exercise your responses.

11. ** Mental Preparation ** - Go into the concession with a positive mindset. Stay calm, patient, and ready to acclimatize as the concession unfolds.

  The further through your pre-negotiation exploration and medication, the more confident and adaptable you will be during the factual concession, adding the chances of achieving your asked   issues.

SETTING CLEAR OBJECTIVES

  Setting clear Objects is essential for success in any shot, icing focus and purposeful action. also is a breakdown

1. ** description ** objects are specific, measurable issues or pretensions you want to achieve within a set timeframe.

2. ** particularity **

-   fluently define what you want to achieve. Avoid vague objects. - rather of" I want to improve deals," use" I want to increase deals by 15% in the coming quarter."

 3. ** Measurability ** ensure that the ideal can be quantified or estimated.

-Use criteria or pointers that can easily show progress or completion.

4. ** Attainability **

- Set objects that are challenging yet attainable. Unrealistic pretensions can be demotivating.

5. ** connection **- ensure that your objective aligns with broader pretensions or the charge of your association or design.

 - Ask if the ideal will move you in the right direction.

6. ** Time- bound **- Assign a clear deadline or timeframe for completion.

- This creates urgency and aids in tracking progress.

7. ** Prioritize **

-If you have multiple objects, rank them predicated on significance or sequence of execution.

- This helps in allocating resources and focus.

 8. ** Break it Down **

- For larger objects, break them into lower, more manageable tasks or milestones. This makes execution easier and provides interim points of achievement.

9. ** Stakeholder Alignment **

- If your objective impacts others or requires their collaboration, ensure everyone involved understands and is aligned with the thing.
10. ** Regular Review **
- Periodically assess your progress towards the ideal.
- Acclimate strategies or tactics if necessary to stay on course.
11. ** Visualization **
-Visual aids like charts, graphs, or boards can help in tracking progress and keeping the objective top of mind.
12. ** Commitment **
- Be wedded to your ideal. Write it down, partake it with others if applicable, and remind yourself of its significance regularly. Setting clear objects provides direction, focus, and a standard for measuring success. When objects are clear and well-defined, sweats are more likely to be purposeful, and issues are more predictable and satisfactory.

THE ART OF ASKING QUESTIONS EASILY!

The art of asking questions involves casting inquiries that elicit meaningful information, promote dialogue, and encourage deeper understanding. also is a breakdown
1. ** Curiosity ** Approach questions with genuine interest and a desire to learn. Curiosity drives meaningful exchanges.
 2. ** Open- ended Questions *
   - Ask questions that requires a fluent answer; either "Yes" or "No"
   - These questions helps you gain knowledge and details about the discussion at hand.
3. ** Clarity ** Expression questions fluently and curtly to avoid confusion or misapprehension.
4. ** listening ** Pay close attention to the response. Effective questioning involves active listening to understand the speaker's perspective fully.
5. ** Probing Questions **- After entering an original response, ask follow- up questions to claw deeper into the content. - This uncovers bolstering provocations, passions, and fresh perceptivity.
6. ** Empathy ** Frame questions with perceptivity to the other person's heartstrings and exploits.
7. ** Neutral Tone **- Ask questions without projecting bias or judgment.
-This creates a safe space for open communication.

8. ** Sequential Structure **- launch with broader questions to establish terrain and gradually move to more specific bones
- This helps in erecting a comprehensive understanding.
9. ** Avoid hypotheticals **
    -   Don't make assumptions before asking question
- Let the person respond in their own words.
10. ** Reflective Questions **
- Mirror back what the person said to show that you've understood and to encourage them to unfold further.
11. ** Timing **
- Ask questions when the person is ready and open to answering.
- Avoid interrupting or asking sensitive questions at unhappy moments.
12. ** Purposeful Intent **-
 Understand why you're asking the question and what information you hope to gain.
 - This ensures your questions contribute to the discussion's purpose.
 13. ** Building Rapport **
-Asking particular or reflective questions can help build trust and fellowship over time.
14. ** Avoid Rapid Fire **
- Give the person time to respond before jumping to the coming question.
- Rushing can make them feel pressured and hinder thoughtful responses.
15. ** Feedback **
- occasionally ask for feedback on your questioning style to improve your communication chops. Asking questions is a skill that can be honed over time. It fosters connection, deepens connections, and facilitates the exchange of precious information.

PSYCHOLOGY AND NEGOTIATION

 The intersection of psychology and negotiation is rich and multifaceted. Here's an exploration of this topic:

1. **Perception:**
   - How negotiators see the situation, their counterparts, and themselves plays a crucial role. Cognitive biases, such as confirmation bias or anchoring, can influence decisions and behaviors during negotiations.

2. **Emotional Intelligence:**
   - Recognizing, understanding, and managing one's own emotions, as well as reading and influencing others' emotions, are pivotal in negotiation.

3. **Trust:**
   - Trust is foundational. Psychological factors like past experiences, stereotypes, and first impressions can impact trust-building.

4. **Reciprocity:**
   - People tend to respond in kind. If one party makes a concession, the other is more likely to reciprocate, driven by a psychological need for balance.

5. **Commitment and Consistency:**
   - People desire to appear consistent in their words and actions. Once someone commits to a stance, they are psychologically more inclined to stick with it.

6. **Social Proof:**
   - Individuals often look to the behaviors of others to guide their own actions. If a negotiation strategy or tactic is seen as standard or accepted by peers, others are more likely to adopt it.

7. **Loss Aversion:**
   - Psychologically, people feel the pain of a loss more acutely than the pleasure of a gain. Understanding this can inform negotiation strategies.

8. **Reactive Devaluation:**
   - Offers made by adversaries are sometimes devalued simply because of who proposed them, regardless of their objective merit.

9. **Framing:**
   - The way information is presented (or framed) can influence decisions. For instance, emphasizing potential gains versus potential losses can elicit different reactions.

10. **Cognitive Dissonance:**

- This occurs when someone holds contradictory beliefs or attitudes. In negotiations, creating cognitive dissonance can be a tactic to prompt reconsideration or change.

11. **Empathy and Perspective-Taking:**
   - Being able to see the situation from the other party's viewpoint can lead to more collaborative outcomes.

12. **Sunk Cost Fallacy:**
   - Individuals often factor in past investments (time, money) when making decisions, even if those investments are no longer relevant. This can hinder rational decision-making in negotiations.

13. **Role of Stress and Fatigue:**
   - Psychological states like stress or fatigue can influence a negotiator's patience, judgment, and decision-making.

14. **Importance of Rapport:**
   - Establishing a positive interpersonal connection can lead to smoother negotiations and more win-win outcomes.

Understanding the psychological mechanisms at play during negotiations allows individuals to better navigate the process, predict potential challenges, and optimize outcomes. Recognizing these elements can lead to more effective, strategic, and empathetic negotiation practices.

CHAPTER FOUR

THE ROLE OF EMOTION

Passions, the intricate shade of heartstrings that color our exploits, play an unarguable part in shaping our conduct, opinions, and relations. They serve as our inner compass, constantly guiding us instinctively through the myriad complications of life. While some might argue that passions are secondary to sense in decision- making processes, the profound influence of our heartstrings on our studies, conduct, and perceptions can't be understated. From the swell of provocation drawn from joy, to the paralyzing grip of fear, to the ground- structure eventuality of empathy, passions are not just flash countries of being; they are important drivers of mortal behavior . Understanding their part is vital not only for particular soul- searching but also for navigating social topographies, erecting connections, and fostering effective communication. Diving deeper into the realm of passions reveals a spectrum so vast that it encapsulates the substance of humanity. Every emotional response, whether it be a temporary sensation or a profound feeling, stems from a myriad of factors our formerly exploits, cultural backgrounds, particular beliefs, and indeed natural tendencies. In the professional sphere, recognizing and managing passions becomes consummate for leaders and armies likewise. Emotional intelligence — the capability to discern and respond to one's own and others' passions has surfaced as a pivotal faculty in the modern factory. It fosters collaboration, rigidity, and severity, traits increasingly recognized as vital in a swiftly changing world. Beyond the factory, passions deeply impact our particular connections. They guide our attachments, produce bonds of trust, and sometimes, unfortunately, lead to conflicts. Yet, indeed in disagreement, understanding the emotional swings can pave the way for concession and collaborative respect. Likewise, in a broader societal terrain, passions drive movements, spark inventions, and indeed impact profitable trends. From the swoon that powers consumer confidence to the cooperative grief that unites communities in the face of tragedy, the part of passions in shaping societies is profound. In essence, to grasp the part of passions is to understand the mortal experience in its wholeness. As we continue to navigate the complications of life, the lens of emotion provides invaluable perceptivity, allowing us to connect, grow, and evolve.

COGNITIVE IMPULSES IN CONCESSION

Cognitive impulses can significantly impact the process and issues of lodgment , constantly leading to fallacious opinions or misinterpretations. also is a concise breakdown of some prominent cognitive impulses in concession
1. ** Anchoring Bias **
- Tendency to calculate heavily on the first piece of information entered(the" anchor") when making opinions. In lodgment , the original offer constantly acts as an anchor, impacting posterior exchanges.
2. ** substantiation Bias **
- The tendency to search for, interpret, and flash back information in a way that confirms one's prepositions. This can lead to overlooking important details that contradict our beliefs.
3. ** Overconfidence Bias **

- overestimating one's knowledge, capacities, or the delicacy of prognostications. This can lead to unrealistic prospects in lodging .

 4. ** Endowment Effect **

- Valuing commodities further largely simply because one owns it. merchandisers, for example, might overestimate what they're dealing with due to this bias.

5. ** Loss Aversion **

- Feeling the pain of a loss more acutely than the pleasure of an original gain. This can make parties trouble-antipathetic, hindering concessions.

 6. ** Reactive Devaluation **

- Automatically cheapen an offer just because it came from the opposing party.

7. ** Status Quo Bias **

- Preferring goods to stay the same or perceiving a change from birth as a loss. This can make parties resistant to change.

8. ** Escalation of Commitment **

- Continuing a behavior or shot as a result of previously invested resources(time, capitalist, or trouble), indeed when it might not be in one's swish interest.

9. ** Sunk Cost falseness **

- Making opinions predicated on former investments rather than considering the implicit future value.

10. ** Vacuity Heuristic **

- counting on immediate samples or recent exploits when assessing a specific content, generality, or decision, which might not represent the broader picture.

11. ** Framing Effect **

-Being told by the way information is presented(framed) rather than the information itself. For example, framing a choice in terms of implicit earnings versus implicit losses can lead to different opinions.

12. ** Reciprocity Bias **

- Feeling obliged to return a favor when someone does a commodity for us, indeed in lodgment . By recognizing and understanding these cognitive impulses, intercessors can more navigate the pitfalls of exorbitant, avoid implicit misapprehensions, and strive for farther ideal and fruitful concession issues.

BUILDING TRUST AND RAPPORT

Building trust and fellowship are foundational rudiments in successful connections, collaborations, and accommodations. Then there is a companion

1. ** Active harkening** - Pay genuine attention when others speak, showing them that you value their perspective. This goes beyond just hearing words; it's about understanding and admitting the passions and provocations behind them.

2. ** trustability **
 - Be harmonious in your actions.However, ensure you follow through, If you make a pledge. thickness establishes pungency and trust.

 3. ** Open Communication **
 - Speak openly about your studies, passions, and enterprises, and encourage others to do the same. translucency minimizes misconstructions.

 4. ** Empathy **
 - Portray a sincere concern towards others. By understanding and admitting their passions, you foster emotional connection.

 5. ** Seek Common Ground **
- Identify participating interests or guests as a foundation for a relationship.

6. ** Respect Boundaries **
 - Understand and respect particular and professional boundaries. This demonstrates respect for the existent's autonomy and comfort.

7. ** Admit miscalculations **
   - Humility, and accept your mistakes. Apologizing and taking responsibility can strengthen trust.

 8. ** Ask Relevant questions**
- Encourage discussion by asking questions that bear further than a' yes' or' no' response. This demonstrates interest.

9. ** Show Appreciation **
 - Fete and recommend others' sweets and benefactions. Everyone values acknowledgment.

 10. ** Maintain Eye Contact **
- While artistic morals can vary, in numerous societies, applicable eye contact during exchanges signals alertness and sincerity.

11. ** Be Authentic ** - Be yourself. Authenticity fosters genuine connections, whereas pretense can frequently be detected, leading to mistrust.

12. ** Seek Feedback **- Regularly ask for feedback on your relations and be open to making adaptations. This shows that you value nonstop enhancement in your connections.

 13. ** Shared gests **

- Engaging in common conditioning, whether it's a work design, a lunch spin, or a platoon- structure event, can strengthen bonds.

14. ** Confidentiality **

- Respect and maintain confidentiality. This is pivotal for trust, especially when sensitive information is involved.   Structure trust and fellowship does not happen overnight. It's a nonstop process, cultivated through harmonious positive relations and genuine collective respect. When trust and fellowship are established, they pave the way for further meaningful, productive, and fulfilling connections.

TACTICS AND WAYS

Tactics and ways are strategies used in colorful fields, from concession to deals to competitive games, to achieve asked   issues. Then there is a broad overview of some common tactics and ways

1. ** The Foot- in- the- Door fashion **

- launch by getting a person to agree to a small request which paves the way for larger requests later.

2. ** Door- in- the- Face fashion **

- Begin with a large request that is anticipated to be refused, followed by a much lower request. The lower request is what you were actually hoping for.

3. ** Anchoring **

- launch with an original, frequently extreme, position(the" anchor"). Any posterior shifts from this position can feel small by comparison, guiding the outgrowth in the asked direction.

4. ** reflecting **

- Subtly mimic the body language, tone, or speech patterns of your counterpart. This can make fellowship and make the other person feel understood.

5. ** The Salami fashion **

- Divide and conquer by addressing issues piece by piece(like slices of salami), rather than dividing everything as before.

6. ** The Decoy Effect **

- Offer another option that makes the bone you want to push appear more seductive. This is frequently used in pricing strategies.

7. ** Deadline fashion **

- Set a time constraint to add pressure and prompt hastily opinions or concessions.

8. ** Good Bobby/ Bad Bobby **
- In a concession, one person takes a tough station, while another is more accommodating. This can make the "good bobby" feel more reasonable by comparison, indeed if their offer is still in their favor.
9. ** Nibble **
 - After agreeing on main terms, ask for a small fresh concession, frequently at the last nanosecond. This can squeeze in redundant benefits.
 10. ** Lowball **
 - Offer a veritably seductive deal to get an original commitment, also change the conditions for some reason, counting on the other party's commitment bias.
11. ** BATNA(Best Alternative to a Negotiated Agreement) **
 - Understand your stylish volition if the current concession fails. This gives you influence and a clearer understanding of when to walk down.
 12. ** High Ground Maneuver **
- Take an innocently or immorally superior position to steer the concession or debate in your favor.
 13. ** pretending **
- Pretend to hold a position or have information that you do not actually retain. It's a perilous tactic and can boomerang if discovered.
 14. ** likening **
- If you are aiming for a middle ground, start high(or low, depending on the environment), awaiting the other party to fight with a lower(or advanced) offer. The stopgap is to end up where you originally aimed.
15. ** Trial Balloons **
- Float an idea without officially committing to it to see the response it garners. When using these tactics and ways, it's important to exercise ethical judgment and maintain integrity. Over-reliance on manipulative tactics can damage long- term connections and character.

Paula J. Albano

CHAPTER FIVE

THE POWER OF SILENCE

In the cacophony of modern life, where words often flood our senses through endless conversations, media, and technology, the potency of silence is frequently underestimated. Yet, within its quietude lies a profound strength. Silence, devoid of noise or distraction, invites introspection, fosters deeper understanding, and communicates in ways words often cannot. It offers a space for reflection, healing, and genuine connection, transcending the boundaries of spoken language. Whether used as a tool in negotiation, a moment of meditation, or a means to absorb the world's subtle wonders, silence possesses an intrinsic power that, when harnessed, can transform interactions, perceptions, and even one's inner self.

Delving deeper, silence isn't merely the absence of sound, but a realm of possibility and revelation. In its embrace, we often find clarity that gets overshadowed by the relentless hum of daily life. Conversations punctuated with moments of silence allow for the digestion of thoughts, giving room for more meaningful exchanges. In negotiations, a well-timed pause can exert pressure, prompt introspection, or emphasize a point more potently than a flurry of words.

Beyond its utility, silence has spiritual and emotional dimensions. Many cultures and philosophies advocate for silent retreats, periods where individuals detach from the external world to journey inward. In these quiet moments, one can grapple with profound questions, soothe inner turmoil, or simply marvel at the vastness of existence.

Furthermore, the power of silence extends to our relationship with the environment. In the quietude of nature—away from the urban din—silence allows us to connect with the rhythms of the Earth, reminding us of our intrinsic bond with the world around us.

However, it's essential to recognize that not all silences are equal. While its power can heal and enlighten, silence can also be a mask for suppression or isolation. It's the quality and intent behind the silence that defines its impact.

In embracing the power of silence, we unlock a deeper realm of connection, understanding, and self-awareness, enriching our experiences and interactions in an increasingly noisy world.

THE ANCHORING EFFECT

Here's a breakdown of the "Anchoring Effect"

The anchoring effect is a cognitive bias wherein individuals rely heavily on the first piece of information they encounter (the "anchor") when making decisions. In the realm of negotiations, this phenomenon plays a critical role, often influencing the trajectory and outcomes of the discussion.

1. **First Impressions Matter:**
   - The initial offer in a negotiation often sets a reference point. Subsequent counteroffers and discussions tend to revolve around this anchor, even if it's arbitrary or significantly skewed.

2. **Power of Suggestion:**

- Even if the anchor is not explicitly used as a bargaining tool, merely mentioning a number or term can influence subsequent evaluations and decisions.

3. **Strategy Implications:**
   - Recognizing the power of anchoring, negotiators often use a high (or low, depending on context) initial offer to frame the negotiation in their favor. The hope is that even after concessions, the final agreement will be closer to their desired outcome.

4. **Overcoming the Bias:**
   - Being aware of the anchoring effect is the first step to mitigating its influence. It's essential to evaluate offers based on their intrinsic merit and external benchmarks rather than relative to the anchor.
   - Researching and having a clear understanding of the market value or precedent for what's being negotiated can help in resisting the anchoring effect.

5. **Double-Edged Sword:**
   - While anchoring can be a potent tool, it can backfire if the initial offer is perceived as extreme or in bad faith. This can lead to mistrust or stalling the negotiation.

6. **Subtle Anchors:**
   - Sometimes, even casual remarks or information shared in passing can act as anchors, subtly influencing perceptions and decisions.

7. **Re-anchoring:**
   - If one feels trapped by an unfavorable anchor, introducing new data, perspectives, or reframing the discussion can help in setting a new, more favorable anchor.

In the dance of negotiation, understanding the anchoring effect is crucial. By recognizing its influence and using it judiciously, negotiators can steer discussions towards favorable outcomes while maintaining trust and credibility.

THE BATNA

In the intricate world of negotiations, having a fallback plan is not just wise but often crucial. This is where the concept of BATNA—or the Best Alternative to a Negotiated Agreement—comes into play.

1. **Definition:**
   - BATNA refers to the most advantageous alternative that a negotiating party can pursue if negotiations fail and no agreement can be reached.

2. **Importance of BATNA:**
   - **Leverage:** Knowing your BATNA gives you power. If the ongoing negotiation is less favorable than your BATNA, you have the confidence to walk away.
   - **Objective Benchmark:** It serves as an objective standard against which any potential negotiated agreement can be gauged.
   - **Reduced Pressure:** When negotiators know their alternatives, they can negotiate with less pressure, as they're not cornered into accepting unfavorable terms.

3. **Identifying Your BATNA:**
   - Conduct thorough research and analysis to identify all possible alternatives should the negotiation fall through.
   - Evaluate each alternative's feasibility and potential outcomes.
   - Choose the alternative that offers the most value as your BATNA.

4. **Strengthening Your BATNA:**
   - Before and during negotiations, look for ways to improve your alternatives, thereby enhancing your negotiating position.

5. **Strategic Use of BATNA:**
   - **Disclosure:** Revealing your BATNA can be a strategic move, especially if it's strong. It can prompt the other party to offer better terms.
   - **Concealment:** If your BATNA is weak, it might be wise not to disclose it, as it could embolden the other party.

6. **Pitfalls to Avoid:**
   - **Overconfidence:** Just because you have a strong BATNA doesn't mean you should neglect the potential benefits of the current negotiation.

- **Misassessment:** Incorrectly evaluating your BATNA can lead to missed opportunities or accepting unfavorable terms.

7. **BATNA vs. WATNA:**
   - While BATNA focuses on the best alternative, it's also valuable to understand your Worst Alternative to a Negotiated Agreement (WATNA). Knowing the worst-case scenario can inform the level of risk in your decision-making.

8. **Negotiating Without a BATNA:**
   - If you don't have a good BATNA, it's crucial to either develop one or proceed with caution, ensuring you're not overly dependent on a single negotiation outcome.

In essence, BATNA is more than just a safety net; it's a tool that empowers negotiators, providing clarity, confidence, and strategic direction. By understanding and leveraging their BATNA, negotiators can navigate discussions with a clear sense of their position and make more informed decisions.

CHAPTER SIX

NEGOTIATION IN PRACTICE

In the vast tapestry of human interactions, negotiation stands out as a critical and intricate dance of communication. Whether it's multinational corporations finalizing a merger, diplomats forging peace treaties, or individuals deciding on the terms of a house purchase, negotiation permeates every stratum of our society. While the theoretical aspects of negotiation offer a foundation, it's in practice that these principles come alive, adapting to the fluidity and unpredictability of real-world scenarios. Every negotiation brings with it unique dynamics, influenced by the parties involved, their interests, the surrounding environment, and a myriad of other factors. In the crucible of actual negotiations, theory meets emotion, strategy confronts spontaneity, and objectives grapple with unforeseen challenges. Exploring negotiation in practice is an expedition into the heart of human decision-making, relationships, and the delicate balance between competition and collaboration.

CASE STUDIES: STRATEGIC NEGOTIATION WINS

Here are three case studies that highlight strategic negotiation wins:
1. **Negotiating the Release of American Hikers - 2011**

Background: In July 2009, three American hikers were arrested in Iran for allegedly crossing into Iranian territory. They were held in captivity for over two years.

Strategic Move: The Sultan of Oman played an instrumental role as an intermediary. Recognizing the importance of trust, Oman discreetly negotiated with Iran, emphasizing goodwill and the humanitarian aspect of the situation. This strategy circumvented the political tension between the U.S. and Iran.

Outcome: In September 2011, following these negotiations and reportedly after Oman paid bail, the hikers were released. This case demonstrates the power of third-party intermediaries and the importance of trust in negotiations.

2. **NBA Player Contract Negotiations - 2020**

Background: Star NBA player was entering free agency and sought a max contract with his current team.

Strategic Move: Instead of merely focusing on the salary, the player and his agent leveraged his brand value, showcasing how he brought more ticket sales, merchandise revenue, and sponsorships. They also negotiated a clause that allowed the player to opt-out if certain conditions, like making the playoffs or building a championship-caliber team, weren't met.

Outcome: The player received a max contract with favorable terms, ensuring he was compensated for his performance and had the flexibility for future career decisions. This strategy underscored the importance of leveraging one's unique value in negotiations.

3. **Dayton Agreement - 1995**

Background: The Bosnian War, a complex conflict involving Bosnia and Herzegovina, Croatia, and Serbia, lasted from 1992 to 1995.

Strategic Move: The U.S. initiated a peace process that culminated in a 21-day negotiation session in Dayton, Ohio. Recognizing the challenges, negotiators isolated the key players from external influences, brought in experts to provide insights on specific issues, and used a mix of bilateral and multilateral discussions to build consensus.

Outcome: The Dayton Agreement was signed in December 1995. The war ended, and Bosnia and Herzegovina was preserved as a single state, but divided into two autonomous entities. The negotiation showcased the efficacy of sustained engagement, expert input, and creating the right environment for dialogue.

Each of these case studies emphasizes different elements of strategic negotiations – the value of third-party intermediaries, understanding and leveraging unique value, and the importance of the negotiation environment and process.

CHALLENGES IN REAL-WORLD SCENARIOS

Real- world accommodations, whether they take place in the boardroom, during political addresses, or in diurnal life, are fraught with challenges. Then are some common challenges faced during accommodations

1. ** Differing Interests and objects ** frequently, parties come into a concession with different pretensions. This divergence can make changing a common ground delicate.

2. ** Cultural and Language walls **Cross-border or transnational accommodations may involve parties from different artistic backgrounds, which can lead to misconstructions if artistic morals and values aren't considered.

3. ** Emotional Attachments ** Occasionally, accommodations come in particular, and feelings can cloud judgment, leading tosub-optimal issues.

4. ** Information Asymmetry ** One party might have further information than the other, creating a power imbalance or causing distrust.

5. ** Time Constraints ** Deadlines can ply pressure, which might lead to hasty opinions or stymie the process of reaching a comprehensive agreement.

6. ** Character and History ** Once relations and established reports can impact current negotiations.However, it can be grueling to overcome, If there is a history of distrust or conflict.

7. ** Multiple Stakeholders ** Accommodations that involve multiple stakeholders can be complex, as the requirements and wants of each stakeholder have to be taken into consideration.

8. ** Legal and Regulatory Challenges ** Especially in transnational business deals, understanding and navigating different legal systems and regulations can be grueling .

9. ** Communication walls ** misconstructions can arise due to unclear communication, leading to confusion and potentially derailing accommodations.

10. ** Zero- Sum Mindset ** The belief that for one party to win, the other must lose, can help palm- palm results and hamper collaboration.

11. ** Fear of Setting Precedents ** Parties might repel agreeing to certain terms out of concern that it'll set a precedent for unborn accommodations.

12. ** External Pressures and Influences ** Outside parties, public opinion, or unlooked-for events can impact a concession, adding layers of complexity.

Navigating these challenges requires medication, understanding, tolerance, and frequently a combination of political and strategic thinking. Effective mediators aren't just complete at the mechanics of concession but also professed at understanding and maneuvering through these real- world challenges.

CHAPTER SEVEN

NEGOTIATING IN DIFFERENT CONTEXTS:

Here's a brief overview of negotiating in different contexts:
1. **Business Negotiations**:
   - **Objective**: Reach mutual agreements, often financial or contractual.
   - **Strategy**: Thorough research, understanding market value, understanding the needs and priorities of both parties.
   - **Key Point**: Be prepared to make concessions but also know your bottom line.

2. **Diplomatic/International Negotiations**:
   - **Objective**: Achieve political or economic agreements between nations.
   - **Strategy**: Diplomacy, understanding cultural nuances, and the political landscape.
   - **Key Point**: National interests come first; patience is critical as these negotiations can be lengthy.

3. **Family and Personal Negotiations**:
   - **Objective**: Reach mutual understanding or solve a dispute.
   - **Strategy**: Active listening, empathy, and seeking win-win solutions.
   - **Key Point**: Relationships matter. It's essential to ensure that the relationship remains intact or improves post-negotiation.

4. **Job Interviews/Salary Negotiations**:
   - **Objective**: Secure a job position or a particular salary/benefits package.
   - **Strategy**: Showcase your value, have an understanding of industry standards, and be prepared to discuss your contributions and accomplishments.
   - **Key Point**: Highlight mutual benefits; make the employer see the value in investing in you.

5. **Customer Service Negotiations**:
   - **Objective**: Resolve customer issues while maintaining company interests.
   - **Strategy**: Active listening, problem-solving, and offering alternatives.

- **Key Point**: Customer retention is vital; sometimes, it's better to make a small concession to ensure a long-term relationship.

6. **Real Estate Negotiations**:
   - **Objective**: Buy or sell property at an advantageous price.
   - **Strategy**: Understand market trends, have clear valuation metrics, and be prepared for counter-offers.
   - **Key Point**: It's not just about price; terms, timing, and contingencies can also be significant negotiating points.

7. **Conflict Resolution**:
   Objective: Resolve a dispute or conflict.
   - **Strategy**: Mediation, seeking understanding, and finding common ground.
   - **Key Point**: The goal is often to find a middle ground where both parties feel their concerns are addressed.

Understanding the context is crucial when entering any negotiation. Tailoring your approach based on the situation can greatly increase your chances of success.

BUSINESS AND CORPORATE SETTINGS

Here's a brief overview of various business and corporate settings:

1. **Startups- **Characteristics**: Newly established businesses, often focused on unique ideas or innovative solutions.
   - **Environment**: Dynamic, high risk, often resource-constrained but with a potential for high reward.
   - **Key Challenges**: Funding, scalability, and market validation.

2. **Small to Medium Enterprises (SMEs)**:
   - **Characteristics**: Established businesses with a moderate number of employees and turnover.
   - **Environment**: Stable compared to startups, with established customer bases and more defined internal processes.

- **Key Challenges**: Growth, competition, and resource management.

3. **Multinational Corporations (MNCs)**:
   - **Characteristics**: Companies that operate in multiple countries.
   - **Environment**: Complex, with various operational bases, diverse workforces, and global supply chains.
   - **Key Challenges**: Regulatory compliance across countries, cultural nuances, and international competition.

4. **Franchises**:
   - **Characteristics**: Business model where individuals buy the rights to open and run a branch of a larger company.
   - **Environment**: Structured, with the franchisee following established business models and guidelines set by the franchisor.
   - **Key Challenges**: Maintaining brand consistency, managing franchisee-franchisor relationships, and local competition.

5. **Family-owned Businesses**:
   - **Characteristics**: Businesses owned and managed by one or more family members.
   - **Environment**: Often more intimate, with family values intertwined with business practices.
   - **Key Challenges**: Succession planning, separating personal and professional matters, and scalability.

6. **Non-profits**:
   - **Characteristics**: Organizations that operate for a cause rather than for profit.
   - **Environment**: Driven by mission and impact, often relying on donations, grants, or volunteers.
   - **Key Challenges**: Fundraising, resource allocation, and maintaining donor trust.

7. **Conglomerates**:
   - **Characteristics**: Large corporations that are made up of diverse, often unrelated businesses.
   - **Environment**: Diverse, with different sectors or industries under one umbrella entity.

- **Key Challenges**: Managing diverse business units, inter-departmental coordination, and central decision-making.

8. **Government-owned Corporations**:
   - **Characteristics**: Entities owned or controlled by the government.
   - **Environment**: Subject to public scrutiny, often having social objectives alongside business goals.
   - **Key Challenges**: Bureaucracy, public perception, and regulatory compliance.

Each business setting has its dynamics, challenges, and operational methodologies. Recognizing and understanding these differences is essential for professionals navigating the corporate world, investors evaluating opportunities, or entrepreneurs considering their best fit.

DIPLOMACY AND INTERNATIONAL RELATIONS IN EVERYDAY LIFE

All consumers often benefit from a wider variety of products at competitive prices.

2. **Travel and Tourism**:
   - Visa requirements, which determine how easily one can visit another country, are a direct result of diplomatic relations. Good bilateral relations often lead to relaxed visa norms.

3. **Cultural Exchange**:
   - International film festivals, art exhibitions, and cultural exchange programs are often supported or facilitated by diplomatic initiatives, allowing people to experience global cultures without leaving their hometown.

4. **Safety and Security**:
   - Diplomatic ties often influence international cooperation in combating global threats like terrorism, piracy, or transnational crimes, indirectly impacting our safety.

5. **Environmental Cooperation**:

- Collaborative international efforts to combat climate change, preserve biodiversity, or address other environmental issues can affect local environmental policies and quality of life.

6. **Technology and Innovation**:
- International partnerships in science and technology can lead to advancements in healthcare, communications, and other sectors that we use daily.

7. **Education**:
- Student exchange programs, international scholarships, and collaborations between universities from different countries offer students opportunities for global exposure.

8. **Healthcare**:
- International collaboration in healthcare research, such as during pandemics, affects the speed and efficiency with which solutions (like vaccines) are developed and distributed.

9. **News and Media**:
- The state of international relations often shapes the news narratives we consume daily, influencing our perception of global events.

10. **Human Rights and Values**:
- Diplomatic pressures and international conventions can influence national policies related to human rights, gender equality, and freedom of expression, impacting societal norms and values.

In essence, while diplomacy and international relations might seem like high-level political activities reserved for politicians and ambassadors, their effects trickle down to influence various aspects of our daily lives. From the products we buy to the news we consume, the state of global relationships plays a pivotal role.

CHAPTER EIGHT

DIGITAL AGE NEGOTIATIONS:

1. **Remote Negotiations**:
   - With platforms like Zoom, Microsoft Teams, or Skype, negotiations are no longer limited by geography.
   - **Challenges**: Overcoming tech glitches, ensuring secure communication, and managing the absence of physical cues.

2. **Use of Data Analytics**:
   - Enhanced data collection and analysis tools enable negotiators to be better informed and to predict trends.
   - **Challenges**: Ensuring data accuracy and dealing with information overload.

3. **Digital Communication Platforms**:
   - Email, instant messaging, and other digital communication tools allow for asynchronous negotiations.
   - **Challenges**: Misinterpretations due to the lack of tone or body language, delays in responses, and ensuring confidentiality.

4. **Social Media and Online Presence**:
   - Online reputation and reviews can be used as leverage in negotiations.
   - **Challenges**: Distorting reality, dealing with false information, and managing public relations.

5. **AI and Automation in Negotiations**:
   - Artificial Intelligence tools can simulate negotiation strategies, predict outcomes, and even automate certain negotiation processes.
   - **Challenges**: Ethical concerns, over-reliance on technology, and potential biases in AI algorithms.

6. **E-contracts and Digital Signatures**:
   - Legal agreements are now often signed digitally, speeding up the negotiation closure process.
   - **Challenges**: Ensuring the legality and security of digital signatures and managing electronic contract storage.

7. **Virtual Reality (VR) and Augmented Reality (AR) Negotiations**:
   - VR and AR can simulate face-to-face negotiations in a digital space, enhancing the experience of remote negotiations.
   - **Challenges**: Tech accessibility, ensuring a realistic representation, and managing potential distractions.

8. **Global Accessibility and Diverse Stakeholders**:
   - The digital age allows for easy collaboration with global partners, expanding the pool of potential negotiators and stakeholders.
   - **Challenges**: Managing time zones, cultural nuances, and varied digital literacy levels.

9. **Digital Training and Simulations**:
   - Online courses, simulations, and role-playing platforms offer negotiators opportunities to hone their skills in virtual environments.
   - **Challenges**: Ensuring realistic scenarios and adapting traditional negotiation techniques to digital platforms.

10. **Cybersecurity in Negotiations**:
    - With negotiations happening online, ensuring the security and confidentiality of communication becomes paramount.
    - **Challenges**: Potential hacks, data breaches, and maintaining trust in digital platforms.

In the digital age, while technology offers negotiators powerful tools and unprecedented convenience, it also brings with it a set of challenges. Adapting to this digital transformation and understanding its intricacies is essential for successful negotiations in modern times.

NAVIGATING VIRTUAL NEGOTIATIONS

Certainly! Navigating virtual negotiations effectively requires a unique set of skills and strategies, distinct from traditional face-to-face negotiations. Here's a guide to navigating virtual negotiations:

1. **Preparation**:
   - **Test Your Tech**: Ensure your internet connection is stable, and familiarize yourself with the video conferencing software. Use headphones to minimize background noise.
   - **Research the Counterparty**: With more global accessibility, it's possible you're negotiating with someone from a different cultural background. Be aware of potential cultural nuances.

2. **Setting the Stage**:
   - **Visuals Matter**: Ensure good lighting so you're clearly visible. A neutral background is ideal. Position your camera at eye level.
   - **Minimize Distractions**: Notify others in your vicinity, mute notifications, and close unrelated programs.

3. **Active Communication**:
   - **Clarify and Repeat**: The absence of physical cues can lead to miscommunication. Periodically summarize key points to ensure understanding.
   - **Stay Engaged**: In a virtual setting, it's crucial to show active participation. Nodding, taking notes, and verbal affirmations can indicate attentiveness.

4. **Leveraging Virtual Tools**:
   - **Use Chat and Screen Sharing**: These tools can be used to share documents, clarify points, or highlight specific data.
   - **Record the Session (with permission)**: This can be beneficial for reviewing the discussion and ensuring no points are missed.

5. **Building Rapport**:
   - **Small Talk**: Spend a few minutes at the start to build a personal connection. This can set a positive tone.
   - **Acknowledge the Medium**: Recognizing that virtual negotiations can be challenging and showing flexibility can build goodwill.

6. **Managing Time Zones**:
   - Be considerate of the time differences if you're negotiating with someone from a different part of the world. Use tools like World Time Buddy to find a suitable time for both parties.

7. **Handling Technical Difficulties**:
   - **Stay Calm**: If issues arise, stay composed. It's a common challenge in virtual settings.
   - **Have a Backup**: Whether it's a secondary communication tool or a phone line, have an alternative way to continue the discussion if needed.

8. **Confidentiality and Security**:
   - Use encrypted platforms for negotiations, especially if sharing sensitive information. Make sure both parties understand the importance of confidentiality.

9. **Closing and Follow-up**:
   - **Clear Next Steps**: Conclude with a summary of decisions made and action items.
   - **Send a Recap Email**: A follow-up email with key points and next steps ensures both parties are aligned.

10. **Continuous Improvement**:
   - **Seek Feedback**: After the negotiation, consider seeking feedback on the virtual experience. This can provide insights for improvement in future sessions.

Navigating virtual negotiations requires an understanding of both the technical and interpersonal nuances of the medium. By being prepared, staying adaptable, and using the tools at your disposal effectively, you can ensure a successful outcome.

THE ROLE OF TECHNOLOGY AND AI

Here's an overview on "The Role of Technology and AI" in various sectors and its broader implications:

1. **Healthcare**:

- **Applications**: AI driven diagnostic tools, personalized treatment plans, predictive analytics for patient outcomes, and robotic surgeries.
  - **Implications**: Faster diagnosis, reduced human error, and tailored treatments, but concerns arise around data privacy and over-reliance on machines.

2. **Finance**:
  - **Applications**: Algorithmic trading, fraud detection, credit scoring, and robo-advisors for personal finance.
  - **Implications**: Enhanced market efficiency, improved fraud prevention, but potential for systemic risks and financial exclusions.

3. **Automotive & Transportation**:
  - **Applications**: Self-driving cars, traffic prediction, smart logistics, and predictive maintenance.
  - **Implications**: Potential reduction in accidents and traffic congestion, but ethical concerns around decision-making algorithms and job losses.

4. **E-commerce & Retail**:
  - **Applications**: Personalized shopping recommendations, chatbots for customer service, and inventory management.
  - **Implications**: Enhanced customer experience, increased sales, but concerns about data privacy and reduced human interaction.

5. **Entertainment**:
  - **Applications**: Content recommendation engines (like Netflix or Spotify), virtual reality experiences, and AI-generated music or art.
  - **Implications**: More tailored entertainment experiences but debates around the authenticity of AI-created content.

6. **Education**:
  - **Applications**: Personalized learning paths, AI tutors, predictive analytics for student performance.
  - **Implications**: Enhanced learning experiences, potential reduction in dropout rates, but concerns about data privacy and homogenization of learning.

7. **Manufacturing**:
   - **Applications**: Smart factories, predictive maintenance, quality control, and supply chain optimization.
   - **Implications**: Improved efficiency and reduced costs, but concerns about job displacements.

8. **Agriculture**:
   - **Applications**: Precision agriculture, crop predictions, automated irrigation systems, and pest prediction.
   - **Implications**: Increased crop yields, sustainable farming practices, but concerns about small farmers' adaptability.

9. **Social Media & Communication**:
   - **Applications**: Content filtering, sentiment analysis, and chatbots.
   - **Implications**: Enhanced user experiences, targeted content delivery, but issues of echo chambers, data privacy, and potential misuse.

10. **Research & Development**:
   - **Applications**: Drug discovery, simulation models, and big data analysis.
   - **Implications**: Accelerated discoveries, but potential over-reliance on AI insights.

Broader Implications:
1. **Job Market**: Automation and AI have the potential to displace certain jobs but also create new ones, necessitating a shift in skills and training.
2. **Ethical Concerns**: AI decision-making processes, especially in critical sectors, raise ethical concerns. Bias in AI, accountability, and transparency are major areas of discussion.
3. **Societal Dynamics**: As AI becomes integral to daily life, it influences societal norms, behaviors, and structures, leading to debates on human-machine interactions, dependency, and the potential for AI dominance.

In essence, technology and AI are redefining various facets of industries and our daily lives. While they bring unprecedented advantages, they also come with challenges that need to be addressed to ensure a harmonious and ethical integration into society.

Paula J. Albano

OVERCOMING OBSTACLES IN NEGOTIATION:

Negotiation is a critical skill in both personal and professional contexts, and it's often fraught with obstacles. Here's a guide to overcoming common barriers in negotiations.
1. **Lack of Trust**   - **Solution**: Build rapport, share some information (even if it's non-critical), and stay consistent in your actions and words. Demonstrating reliability over time fosters trust.

2. **Communication Barriers**:
   - **Solution**: Actively listen, ask clarifying questions, and ensure that you are articulate in your responses. Consider potential cultural or language differences and adjust accordingly.

3. **Fixed Pie Perception**:
   - Many negotiations stall because parties believe they're dividing a fixed set of resources.
   - **Solution**: Focus on expanding the pie rather than just dividing it. Look for mutual benefits or trade-offs where both parties can benefit.

4. **Emotional Barriers**:
   - **Solution**: Stay calm and composed, even when faced with aggressive tactics. Practice emotional intelligence to understand and navigate emotions, both yours and your counterpart's.

5. **High Anchoring**:
   - Starting with an extreme initial position can stall negotiations.
   - **Solution**: Be prepared with market values and justifications. Counter with well-researched arguments and remain open to finding middle ground.

6. **Overconfidence**:
   - **Solution**: Always come prepared with data to back up your positions. Also, be willing to listen and adjust based on new information.

7. **Deadline Pressures** - **Solution**: If possible, start negotiations well in advance of any deadlines. If faced with a tight deadline, be transparent about it, as it may foster cooperation.

8. **Cultural Differences**:

- **Solution**: Research and understand the cultural nuances of your counterpart. Respect these differences and, when necessary, employ a mediator familiar with both cultures.

9. **Information Asymmetry**:
   - When one party has more information than the other, it can create an imbalance.
   - **Solution**: Do thorough research beforehand. If caught off guard, consider postponing the negotiation to gather more information.

10. **Fear of Losing**:
   - **Solution**: Re-frame the negotiation as a win-win opportunity rather than a win-lose scenario. Concentrate on the value and benefits for both sides.

11. **Commitment Issues**:
   - Often, parties might agree in principle but hesitate to commit formally.
   - **Solution**: Clearly outline the benefits of the agreement. Consider phased commitments or trial periods to ease concerns.

12. **Lack of Authority**:
   - Sometimes the person you're negotiating with might not have the authority to finalize decisions.
   - **Solution**: Ensure you're speaking to the decision-maker or someone who has the authority to commit.

In essence, successful negotiation isn't just about getting what you want but finding a solution that is acceptable and beneficial for all parties involved. By understanding and overcoming obstacles, you can navigate negotiations more effectively and reach mutually beneficial outcome.

CHAPTER NINE

DEALING WITH DIFFICULT PEOPLE

In the vast theater of life's interactions, navigating the intricate maze of personalities is an ethereal ballet, transcending mere encounters. Difficult people, often perceived as tempests in this dance, are akin to mysterious whirlwinds, embodying both chaos and revelation. Engaging with them is not a mere act of patience, but a deep dive into the oceans of empathy and the unknown. Their complexities become riddles, not to be solved, but to be experienced. Every challenge they pose is an invitation to peer beyond the mundane, into realms where shadows weave tales of unspoken fears and concealed desires. Dealing with them is less about resolution and more about resonance, a cosmic tug of war where one doesn't simply cope, but dances on the edge of understanding and bewilderment. For in this dance, one discovers not just the other, but oneself.In the tapestry of existence, difficult souls emerge as intricate threads, weaving patterns that defy simplicity. They are the stormy seas that test our navigation skills, beckoning us to explore depths beyond the surface. Engaging with them transcends the realm of strategy; it's an art form that demands emotional alchemy. It's like deciphering ancient manuscripts written in emotions rather than words, each interaction a delicate brush stroke on the canvas of connection. These souls are not adversaries, but mirrors reflecting the untamed wilderness within us. To deal with them is to embark on a pilgrimage into the heart's labyrinth, a journey of paradoxes, where every challenge is a hidden invitation to uncover the gems concealed within both them and us.

OVERCOMING DEADLOCKS AND IMPASSES

Deadlocks and impasses can arise in various scenarios, from negotiations and discussions to project management. Here's a guide on overcoming them:

1. **Reassess Objectives**:
   - Both parties should restate their primary objectives. Sometimes, revisiting the main goals can highlight overlooked common ground.

2. **Take a Break**:
   - A short pause can provide an opportunity to regroup, think, and approach the situation with a fresh perspective.

3. **Introduce a Neutral Mediator**:
   - A third-party mediator can offer a fresh perspective, help clarify issues, and guide the discussion towards resolution.

4. **Change the Setting**:

- Moving to a new location or altering the environment can sometimes reset the dynamic and facilitate more productive discussions.

5. **Break Down Larger Issues**:
   - Divide the main point of contention into smaller, more manageable issues. Tackling each smaller problem might pave the way to resolving the larger one.

6. **Find Alternative Solutions**:
   - If the current approach isn't working, brainstorm other possible solutions or compromises.

7. **Prioritize Issues**:
   - Determine which issues are most critical and which ones can be set aside for later discussion.

8. **Use Objective Criteria**:
   - Instead of subjective stances, use data, benchmarks, or other objective criteria to guide decisions.

9. **Seek Mutual Benefits**:
   - Shift the focus from a zero-sum approach to finding solutions that provide mutual benefits.

10. **Acknowledge Emotions**:
   - Addressing and validating any underlying emotions can help clear hurdles. Remember, not all deadlocks are purely based on logical disagreements; emotions can play a significant role.

11. **Reframe the Discussion**:
   - Present the situation or problem in a new light. This can provide a new perspective and reveal solutions that were previously overlooked.

12. **Consider Future Implications**:
   - Reflect on the potential consequences of not reaching an agreement. This can provide motivation to find a resolution.

13. **Use "What If" Scenarios**:

- Propose hypothetical solutions to gauge the other party's reaction without committing to a decision.

14. **Agree to Disagree**:
   - In some cases, it might be best to acknowledge the impasse and decide on the next steps without complete agreement. This can mean postponing the issue, seeking external input, or pursuing separate paths.

Deadlocks and impasses can be frustrating, but they're often an indication of deeply held beliefs or significant stakes for the involved parties. Approaching such situations with patience, empathy, and creativity can pave the way for resolution and mutual understanding.

ETHICAL CONSIDERATIONS:

Ethical considerations underpin many aspects of human interactions and decision-making across diverse sectors. Here's an exploration of ethical considerations in various contexts and their implications:

1. **Business**:
   - **Considerations**: Fair trade, environmental sustainability, fair wages, and transparent advertising.
   - **Implications**: Ethical businesses can build trust with consumers, foster employee loyalty, and have long-term success. However, they might face short-term costs or competitive challenges.

2. **Medicine**:
   - **Considerations**: Informed consent, patient confidentiality, non-maleficence (do no harm), and equitable treatment.
   - **Implications**: Upholding ethical standards ensures patient safety and trust but can sometimes conflict with economic or administrative pressures.

3. **Research**:

- **Considerations**: Honest reporting, protection of human subjects, avoiding plagiarism, and declaring conflicts of interest.

- **Implications**: Ethical research enhances the credibility of findings, though it might require more time and resources.

4. **Technology & AI**:

- **Considerations**: Data privacy, unbiased algorithms, transparency in AI decision-making, and accessibility of technology.

- **Implications**: Ethical tech companies foster user trust, but they might face challenges in balancing innovation, profitability, and ethics.

5. **Environment**:   - **Considerations**: Conservation, sustainable resource use, animal welfare, and intergenerational equity.

- **Implications**: Prioritizing the environment can ensure long-term planetary health but might involve short-term economic sacrifices.

6. **Education**:

- **Considerations**: Equal access to quality education, unbiased evaluations, and fostering critical thinking.

- **Implications**: An ethically-driven education system produces well-rounded, informed citizens, but challenges arise in resource allocation and curriculum decisions.

7. **Law and Governance**:

- **Considerations**: Equitable enforcement of laws, transparency in decision-making, and safeguarding citizens' rights.

- **Implications**: Ethical governance fosters societal trust and stability, though it requires constant vigilance and checks and balances.

8. **Media and Journalism**:

- **Considerations**: Truthful reporting, avoiding sensationalism, respecting privacy, and declaring biases.

- **Implications**: Ethical journalism fosters an informed society but might clash with commercial interests or political pressures.

9. **Finance**:

- **Considerations**: Transparency in transactions, avoiding conflicts of interest, and promoting financial inclusivity.
- **Implications**: Ethical financial practices build investor and consumer trust but may face challenges in highly competitive environments.

10. **Personal Relationships**:
   - **Considerations**: Honesty, respect, consent, and understanding boundaries.
   - **Implications**: Upholding ethical considerations fosters trust and healthy relationships, though it might require difficult conversations and self-reflection.

In essence, ethical considerations serve as a compass guiding individual and collective actions towards a just, fair, and harmonious society. While ethical paths might sometimes seem challenging, they often lead to sustainable, long-term benefits for individuals and communities alike.

CHAPTER TEN

FAIR PLAY AND INTEGRITY

Fair play and integrity are foundational principles in numerous arenas, from sports and games to business and personal relationships. Here's an exploration of these concepts:

1. **Definition**:
   - **Fair Play**: Abiding by rules and acting in an honest, straightforward manner. It involves treating all participants with respect and ensuring an even playing field.
   - **Integrity**: Adherence to moral and ethical principles, emphasizing honesty and consistency of character regardless of the situation or outcome.

2. **Sports**:
   - Athletes are expected to compete honestly, avoiding tactics like doping or cheating. Fair play extends to respecting opponents, officials, and fans.
   - Integrity in sports means playing for the love of the game rather than external rewards. It involves acknowledging mistakes, respecting decisions, and emphasizing teamwork.

3. **Business**:
   - Fair play includes honest advertising, treating employees equitably, and avoiding deceptive practices.
   - Integrity is evident when businesses maintain ethical standards even if it may impact profitability. It's about honoring commitments, being transparent, and building trust.

4. **Education**:
   - Students engage in fair play by avoiding plagiarism or cheating during exams.
   - Integrity in academia means pursuing knowledge genuinely, acknowledging sources, and promoting authentic learning.

5. **Personal Relationships**:

- Fair play involves mutual respect, understanding, and avoiding manipulative behaviors.
- Integrity in relationships translates to being truthful, honoring commitments, and being authentic in one's interactions.

6. **Governance and Politics**:
- Fair play dictates that elections are free and fair, policies are made transparently, and public resources are used equitably.
- Integrity in politics means placing public interest above personal gain, avoiding corruption, and adhering to ethical standards.

7. **Benefits**:
- **Trust**: Both fair play and integrity foster trust among individuals, within communities, and between nations.
- **Stability**: They promote consistent and predictable behaviors, leading to societal stability.
- **Reputation**: Entities that uphold these principles often enjoy enhanced reputations and increased loyalty.

8. **Challenges**:
- **Short-Term Losses**: Upholding integrity might sometimes lead to short-term disadvantages, such as losing a game or missing out on a business opportunity.
- **External Pressures**: Societal, peer, or economic pressures can sometimes challenge the principles of fair play and integrity.

9. **Upholding Fair Play and Integrity**:
- **Education and Training**: Regular training and education can instill these values from a young age.
- **Clear Guidelines**: Whether in sports or business, clear rules and codes of conduct can help in ensuring fair play.
- **Accountability**: Regular checks, balances, and transparent mechanisms to hold violators accountable can promote integrity.

In essence, fair play and integrity serve as guiding lights, ensuring that our actions are consistent with moral and ethical principles. While they might sometimes seem at odds with immediate gains, in the long run, they lead to trust, respect, and sustainable success.

Paula J. Albano

CULTURAL SENSITIVITIES AND GLOBAL PERSPECTIVES

In an increasingly interconnected world, understanding cultural sensitivies and adopting a global perspective are vital for effective communication, collaboration, and coexistence. Here's an exploration of these concepts:

1. **Cultural Sensitivities**:
   - **Definition**: Recognizing, understanding, and respecting the differences and nuances within and between cultures.
   - **Importance**: Helps avoid misunderstandings or offenses, builds trust, and promotes positive interactions across different cultures.

2. **Global Perspectives**:
   - **Definition**: Viewing issues and ideas from a worldwide viewpoint, understanding the interconnectedness of systems, and recognizing the impact of local actions on a global scale.
   - **Importance**: Encourages broad-mindedness, supports global collaboration, and promotes sustainable solutions to worldwide challenges.

3. **Benefits of Cultural Sensitivity & Global Perspective**:
   - **Enhanced Communication**: Enables effective communication with diverse populations, breaking down barriers of misunderstanding.
   - **Inclusive Decision-Making**: Incorporates diverse viewpoints, leading to richer, more informed decisions.
   - **Improved Business Relations**: Allows companies to successfully operate in different cultural markets and appeal to a global audience.
   - **Social Harmony**: Reduces biases, prejudices, and stereotypes, promoting peaceful coexistence.

4. **Challenges**:
   - **Stereotyping**: Making generalized assumptions can lead to misunderstandings.
   - **Overadaptation**: While it's crucial to adapt, losing one's identity or values in the process can be counterproductive.
   - **Language Barriers**: Language nuances can sometimes lead to miscommunications or misconceptions.

5. **Ways to Foster Cultural Sensitivity & Global Perspective**:
    - **Education**: Introduce curricula that covers world history, global challenges, and diverse cultures.
    - **Travel**: Immersing oneself in a new culture can offer firsthand understanding and appreciation of its nuances.
    - **Cultural Exchange Programs**: Engage in programs where individuals can live, work, or study in different countries.
    - **Diverse Media Consumption**: Consuming books, movies, and news from varied sources can help understand global perspectives.
    - **Engage in Discussions**: Talking with individuals from diverse backgrounds can offer fresh viewpoints and insights.
    - **Attend Workshops**: Participate in cultural sensitivity training or global issues seminars.

6. **Practical Applications**:
    - **Business**: Helps in international business relations, negotiations, and marketing strategies tailored for different cultures.
    - **Diplomacy**: Facilitates international relations and the forging of alliances.
    - **Social Work**: Aids in providing care and support to individuals from diverse backgrounds.
    - **Education**: Prepares students for a globalized world and fosters a more inclusive environment.

In essence, cultural sensitivities and a global perspective are not just about recognizing and respecting differences, but about understanding the intricate web of interconnections that bind us all. As our world becomes more globalized, these values will become increasingly vital in shaping a harmonious, collaborative future.

CHAPTER ELEVEN

THE ONGOING JOURNEY OF BECOMING A MASTER NEGOTIATOR

"In the vast tapestry of human interactions, the art of negotiation weaves a mesmerizing tale of ambition, tact, and intuition. To embark on the journey of becoming a master negotiator is to embrace a dance where words become the rhythm and silence, the melody. It's not merely about reaching agreements, but understanding the myriad emotions, desires, and fears that dance behind the eyes of the counterpart. The path is not linear, nor is it defined. Like a river, it meanders through terrains of patience, swirls around boulders of resistance, and occasionally plunges into the waterfalls of breakthroughs. It's an odyssey where mastery isn't an end but a horizon, always just a step beyond, beckoning the seeker to traverse further into the realm of the unsaid and the uncharted.Within the cosmic ballet of human discourse, negotiating becomes an alchemical act, transcending mere transactional exchanges. It's akin to watching two galaxies dance, where words are stars and intentions are the dark matter that holds them in place. A master negotiator doesn't just speak, they listen to the symphony of unspoken sentiments, understanding that beneath the surface lies a universe of dreams, apprehensions, and aspirations. It's a mystical journey, where outcomes aren't just results, but revelations. Every negotiation, a ritual; every conversation, a spell. To become a master is not to conquer, but to surrender to the enigma, allowing oneself to be both the storm and the calm, the question and the answer.

EMBRACING THE POWER OF LIFELONG LEARNING

In the labyrinth of existence, the quintessence of our being is often illuminated by the beacon of knowledge. Embracing lifelong learning is not merely about accumulating facts or mastering skills; it is a profound dance with the unknown. With every step, we unshackle ourselves from the constraints of yesterday, soaring into the vast expanse of the ever-evolving universe of understanding. For in the relentless pursuit of enlightenment, we become both the sculptor and the sculpture, carving our destiny with the chisel of curiosity. Embrace this journey, for it is in the perpetual thirst for knowledge that we truly discover the boundless power of life.

Paula J. Albano

CONCLUSION

"In the intricate dance of human interactions, negotiation stands out as a pivotal tool, a bridge that transforms conflicts into resolutions and ideas into actionable plans. Harnessing the strategic power of negotiation transcends mere transactional exchanges—it's about forging relationships, understanding diverse perspectives, and navigating the intricate nuances of human desires and needs. As global dynamics shift and challenges mount, the ability to negotiate effectively becomes more vital than ever. It's not merely a skill but a craft, refined over time, that holds the potential to shape destinies, influence outcomes, and create harmonious pathways in both personal and global arenas. As we look ahead, embracing the strategic power of negotiation will undoubtedly remain central to progress, understanding, and collaboration in an increasingly interconnected world."p

www.ingramcontent.com/pod-product-compliance
Lightning Source LLC
Chambersburg PA
CBHW071108260726
48661CB00006B/2544